Hi, Parents!

Your child's love of reading starts here, with HarperAlley's **I Can Read Comics!**

I Can Read Comics introduces children to the world of graphic novel storytelling and encourages visual literacy in emerging readers. Comics inspire reader engagement unlike any other format. They ask readers to infer and answer questions, like:

1. What do I read first? Image or text?
2. Why is this word balloon shaped this way, and that word balloon shaped that way?
3. Why is a character making that facial expression? Are they happy, angry, excited, sad?

From the comics your child reads with you to the first comic they read on their own, there are **I Can Read Comics** for every stage of reading:

LEVEL 1
Simple stories for shared reading.

LEVEL 2
Engaging stories for children reading on their own.

LEVEL 3
Complex stories for independent readers.

The magic of graphic novel storytelling lies between the gutters. Unlock the magic with…

I Can Read Comics!

I Can Read *Comics* Cartooning Basics

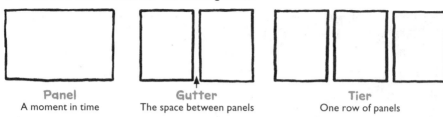

Panel
A moment in time

Gutter
The space between panels

Tier
One row of panels

Word Balloons When someone talks, thinks, whispers, or screams, their words go in here:

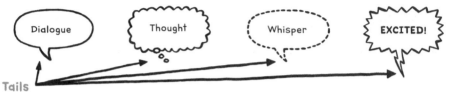

Dialogue
Thought
Whisper
EXCITED!

Tails
Point to whoever is talking / thinking / whispering / screaming / etc.

A quick how-to-read comics guide:

In a **panel**, read the text on the **left** first.

Then, read the text on the **right**.

Remember to...
Read the text along with the image, paying close attention to the character's acting, the action, and/or the scene. Every little detail matters!

No dialogue? No problem!
If there is no dialogue within a panel, take the time to read the image. Visual cues are just as important as text, so don't forget about them!

On a page, **start here**, in the **top left** corner!

After that, read the panel immediately to the **right**.

When you're done up there, come down here and read **this** panel **next**!

ME NEXT! ME NEXT!

You're almost there...

YOU MADE IT! You just read a comic page!

YAY!

For Gabriel, builder of fantastic pillow forts and writer of amazing stories. —K.S.L.

To Aria, Noah, and Sofie. Create a life of wonder! —N.M.

HarperAlley is an imprint of HarperCollins Publishers.
I Can Read® and I Can Read Book® are trademarks of HarperCollins Publishers.

Ty's Travels: Camp-Out
Text copyright © 2023 by Kelly Starling Lyons
Illustrations copyright © 2023 by Niña Mata

Library of Congress Control Number: 2022948790
ISBN (trade bdg.) 978-0-06-308366-0 — ISBN 978-0-06-308365-3 (pbk.)

Book design by Maddy Price
23 24 25 26 27 LB 10 9 8 7 6 5 4 3 2 1 ❖ First Edition

TY'S TRAVELS
Camp-Out

by Kelly Starling Lyons
pictures by Niña Mata

An Imprint of HarperCollinsPublishers

Everyone was excited to go camping, when all of a sudden...

11

13

15

19